LEARNING
TO SEE
IN THREE
DIMENSIONS

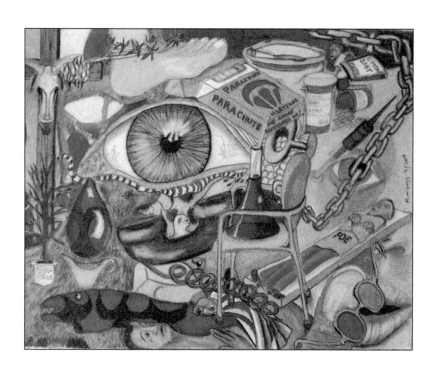

LEARNING TO SEE IN THREE DIMENSIONS

❨

POEMS

Pamela Spiro Wagner

GREEN WRITERS PRESS
& SUNDOG POETRY CENTER

First paperback edition: June 2017.

Green Writers Press is a Vermont-based publisher whose mission is to spread a message of hope and renewal through the words and images we publish. Throughout we will adhere to our commitment to preserving and protecting the natural resources of the earth. To that end, a percentage of our proceeds will be donated to environmental activist groups. Green Writers Press gratefully acknowledges support from individual donors, friends, and readers to help support the environment and our publishing initiative.

Giving Voice to Writers Who Will Make the World a Better Place
Green Writers Press | Brattleboro, Vermont
www.greenwriterspress.com

Sundog Poetry Center
www.sundogpoetry.org

ISBN: 978-0998260464

Cover art and throughout the book © Pamela Spiro Wagner.
Cover art colored pencils on Strathmore Bristol paper.

Sundog Poetry Center will donate 5% of the sales of this book to
Inclusion Center, Brattleboro, Vermont.

PRINTED ON PAPER WITH PULP THAT COMES FROM FSC-CERTIFIED FORESTS, MANAGED FORESTS THAT GUARANTEE RESPONSIBLE ENVIRONMENTAL, SOCIAL, AND ECONOMIC PRACTICES BY LIGHTNING SOURCE. ALL WOOD PRODUCT COMPONENTS USED IN BLACK & WHITE OR STANDARD COLOR PAPERBACK BOOKS, UTILIZING EITHER CREAM OR WHITE BOOKBLOCK PAPER, THAT ARE MANUFACTURED IN THE LAVERGNE, TENNESSEE, PRODUCTION CENTER ARE SUSTAINABLE FORESTRY INITIATIVE® (SFI®) CERTIFIED SOURCING.

To MEH, poet,

who recited miraculous Hopkins and gave me the gift,

to WW, who really saw me,

and who showed me the path to freedom,

and to the miracle that is each one of my friends,

old and new

☾

This book is for you.

TO THE READER . . .

With thanks to Helen Vendler

who may be sitting as I am
in a green recliner with a cup of tea
staring out through the porch
to a darkened streetlamp outside the diner,
with a book in her lap, mine, I hope
the only one I feel I should have to mention
if I mention a book in a poem I write;
to the reader, the nitpicker, the one
who may be wondering why
on p. 47 there are two ands, one
right after another, and whose fault that is;
and to the reader, who may be tired
after a long ride home on the bus
after dark and a meal not worth mentioning
who picks up my book but finds his eyes
closing before he has opened the cover,
I say: Forgive me,
I am only a writer sitting in a green recliner
with a cup of tea, I can't explain
those two ands or the mysterious streetlamp
or warm the feet of a tired reader in his bed.
I can only put music on
and tell him stories to make movies
turn in his head, to let him wake

with the sudden understanding that poetry
may be all it takes to make a life—
well, my life at any rate, and maybe his,
and maybe the nitpicker's and yours, too,
staring through the porch to the streetlamp
where what happens so mysteriously is poetry—
and the whole night is wrapped in the words
spoken by two strangers meeting there
or not spoken, which is poetry too,
and all of us who listen are waiting
for the music of what is to happen.

CONTENTS

SEEING IN THREE DIMENSIONS: SPACE, MATTER, LOVE

"The world is charged with the grandeur of God."
—GERARD MANLEY HOPKINS

As an older adult with severe double vision, no depth perception, and "convergence insufficiency," I saw a special Vision Therapy trained optometrist for about a year. The experience I write about below happened just before I ended treatment.

EARLY ONE MORNING, well before dawn lightened behind the fence of trees to the east, I went to move my snowed-in car to make way for the plows. As the automatic door opened, letting me out into the cold, I could see that falling snow against the street lamps made sparkles and sparks. I headed towards the car, thinking of nothing but the cold. Then, my brain clicked, like the flip of a switch, and something in my vision changed. Instead of seeing the snow fall in a sheet, curtain-like, in front of me as I always had before, I now walked *inside* it, as if in a snow globe, separate flakes plummeting around me, each on a different plane, riding a separate moving point in space as it fell.

Startled, I blinked my eyes, thinking the curtain would close in again. Nothing. I looked down at a snow-covered bush next to me on the sidewalk. The ends of its bare twigs were lightly mounded, contrasts heightened, the whiteness of the snow and twigs gently vibrating with laser-etched clarity and precision of detail. I can only describe what came over me then as a feeling of connectedness, of affection for the universe. I smiled as I stood there, realizing that I was seeing depth, I was seeing *space,* and the spaces between things, for the first time. At least for the first time that I could remember, for the first time since who knows how long. That was all, and it was everything.

I had a dream once that I never forgot, a dream in which I actually ate chocolate. I tasted it and I swallowed it, and in which I stroked a cat and was able even in the dream to feel the soft silkiness of its warm fur. Both of these acts, though in reality mental, not physical, took enormous effort, even courage. I felt, while sleeping, that if I were to break the spell of whatever made these experiences "forbidden," neurologically speaking, *something would happen.* It was not clear to me at the time of this dream whether it would be catastrophic or miraculous, and as a result, while I managed to push through those barriers, even in sleep, my apprehension, indeed my terror, was immense.

This experience in the snow felt very similar. Space, I saw with sudden breath-taking enlightenment, is *not* negative. The "negative space" artists speak so passionately of doesn't exist. Space is real, a solid kind of stuff that gives definition and substance to matter. In fact, if space, the medium that surrounds everything, could have changed the ordinary boxwood in the snow before me into a burning bush of miracles, what couldn't it do?

Now, I admit that contemplation of snow-covered shrubbery and buried cars and yellow street lamps, among other things, in sub-freezing temperatures has never been my favorite way to spend an early morning. Nevertheless, it was a long time before I went indoors. Finally, rubbing my hands to warm them, I made my way to my computer to jot down some notes, and when I put my fingers towards the keyboard. I was immediately taken by the fact that my hands went *outwards* into space. And then the very sight of the keyboard elevation made my heart ache. What could be lovelier than the fact that keys themselves protruded *above* the keyboard? The words were palpable and delicious, not just with possibility but with reality: *outwards, protrude, elevate, above.* My typing fingers hovered in a tangible space over the keys, and I could see that there was a space between my fingers and the keys. Indeed it was a small miracle the way space gave form to those small squares, indented just slightly to fit the pads of my fingertips. All this was too much for me and alone in my room I found myself laughing aloud. Suddenly, the entire world was friendly.

I went around my apartment. *Look at this! Look at that!* I couldn't pry my eyes from things. Dish towels announced themselves, as their threads stood up, cupped and rounded by space, each one loved into being by the fact of the empty air that surrounded it. Folds struck me as the most beautiful objects I had ever seen. Folds in terrycloth fabric differed utterly from folds in other fabrics. Even paper bent around an angle, embracing a fold, allowed sculpted space on each side to nearly bring tears to my eyes. Who would have thought that material, bent, could become a form of such magnificence?

And on it went. Doorknobs yearned, reaching out from doors into space. Bookshelves provided welcoming recesses, intimate and implicit with corners, as if saying, *Come in, we will protect you.* There were delicious concavities in every spoon! My circuit of the room over and over would have been ridiculous, had not everything been so lovely, and so thoroughly devastating.

Snow-covered bushes, computer keyboard, a hand or any nose extended into the air—I understood in an instant that it was space, this lovely *positive* space, that sculpts the entire world, just as a sculptor carves stone. I knew then that it is only because most people get so used to depth perception all their lives that they lose all ability to perceive the beauty of space, to see how much space quite literally embodies.

Later the vision faded and as my eyes relaxed, my ability to see "3-D" was lost. But I still remember, towards the end of the experience, how as I looked into an empty wastebasket I was bowled over to understand that it had a rounded interior. The sheer "interiority" of it, the fact that the space inside it implied roundedness so matter-of-factly that I did not have to *feel* it to know this—why hadn't I understood this before? It struck me as a terrible failure and yet the most transcendent discovery of my life. I knew then that if the world was charged with the grandeur of anything, it must be a positive, optimistic Shaper of things and that this Shaper is the world's—the universe's—Creator, which we instead call, as if it were nothing, "empty space."

Could it be possible that most people will never have an opportunity to experience such overwhelming love for spoons and doorknobs and computer keys or even for hands above the paper or every possible human nose that sticks out into space? If so, it might even be the reason we humans have let ourselves destroy our environment, the most precious matter in the Creative Space around us.

Because we did not understand how space is our Creator, we have destroyed it and ourselves in the process. How could we have done otherwise? We did not know because we could not *see*. And if we could not see, how could we know the truth: that Space *is* Love that creates the world and makes us and all matter beautiful.

Pamela Spiro Wagner

DESIRE AND MEMORY

Artist As Ornament
COLORED PENCIL AND ACRYLIC ON PAPER

MOSAIC

*Mosaic: a word that means from the muses, from Moses
and a work of art created from broken fragments of pottery,
stone or glass.*

Even the first time, surrender was not hard,
though the grownups and mothers
with their drinks and swizzle sticks
undoubtedly thought it so when you volunteered
your only present that 10th Christmas
to a younger child who wouldn't understand
being giftless at the tail end of a line to Santa,
nor your inherent sin in being born.
Such generosity should have stayed
between your concept-of-God and you,
but grownup admiration (you could not hope
to make your act unpublic) sullied the soap
of *any* generosity's power to cleanse you.
Other atonements followed, only one
almost perfect, being perfectly anonymous
spoiled by an accomplice's later telling.
Perfection? You never made that grade,
your terrible love for God demanding all life
from your life. No one told you, "Live a lot,"
not in words that made it matter, though
they doubtless counseled, "Live a little."
You were always in school to be perfect,
never knowing that life is a classroom
where one learns to love flaws
by throwing bad pots, to shatter
them with careful hammer,
assembling beauty from broken things.

She Dreams of Vultures
OIL ON GESSOBORD

COUNTERFACTUALS

*"What is particularly curious about quantum theory
is that there can be actual physical effects arising from . . .
counterfactuals—that is, things that might have happened
although they did not . . .*
                                    —Roger Penrose

1

I didn't marry the right man
for twenty years and now, see
how fat he has grown
against the sickle of my body

he knocks at my bones
asking nothing

2

If he desired only
the weeds in my garden

I would give him
my spine, that knot of pearls
my hair, that blanket

3

In my mouth, ashes,
the bed we share empty
he's not the right man I didn't marry

Rusting in the dark
in the shingled shed

my body thin as a hoe
hangs on the wall
beside his wide shovel

THIS IS NOT AN EPITHALAMION...

which is Greek for an occasional poem
written for a wedding, and though
I have written it for just such an occasion

and it has already mentioned a wedding
and though the wedding happens to be
that of my twin sister and a man I really like

it has none of the elements I think
belong in an epithalamion. For one thing:
it immoderately praises no one. I know

the couple in question too well not to
praise them with accuracy, for all
they are both my heroes. "Adulation"

derives from words that suggest
a dog wagging its tail, the Latin root meaning
"flattery." But flattery flatters no one

so though I adore them both, I will praise them
with moderation, this being after all
no epithalamion. If I extol instead

the steady monogamy of bald eagles,
and beavers, gray wolves and prairie voles,
with their love biochemistry just like our own,

fall-in-love pheromones drawing and binding,
what can I say of these two humans
over-brimming like whooping cranes

with blessing and blessings, who would dance
before dinner each night in their kitchen?
Wisdom fails me, my mouth falls empty.

I offer what I do, what I am: this poem.
So you see, after all, it *is* an epithalamion,
it turns on the point of whooping crane

dancing, on the joy and the blessing,
on hormones and pheromones
and (let us not forget) this wedding.

FOR A FRIEND WHO THINKS
POETRY IS FOR THE BIRDS

In memory of Lynn L

and though *she* may,
this buff-bellied hummingbird nesting
on a clothespin might not mind a poem,
if her nest is left unmolested
till the tablet eggs hatch out safely
and her brood is fledged.
So I'll say, *l'chaim*, and this one is for the birds,
lest I burden my friend with a birthday
who well deserves a poem
but might view being given one
like a social phobic shaking hands or a hug.
And I should know.
And should I prove I'm huggable
if she can tolerate being versed?
Or would we be denying each the need to be
the person she is: that is, the same
as she was yesterday? But that's not need,
just habit—and sometimes
habits, like desire and memory
mix badly, breeding not lilacs but ruts
when shaking things up's the only thing to do,
doing what's needful only,
since change is the only thing
that never changes.
What if I, the non-hugger, who never shakes

a hand, what if I embrace the friend
for whom verse is worse
than a for-the-birds waste of words,
would she accept this gift from me,
though it's (horrors!) a poem?

Tidal Restraint
ACRYLIC ON GESSOBORD

ON FLOOD SEASON AND RUMORS OF LOSS

When springtime brought snowmelt and storms and forecasted floods
and the salesmen refused to return my frantic calls about flood

insurance, I threw caution to the April winds and my cat into the river
in my dream and my dreamed-cat swam, caught fish in the rising river,

and ate forever, sleek, fat and mackerel happy.
It was I, in truth, who was unhappy.

If floods be told as a truth of what matters most
my cat could fend for herself in most matters

whether or not she could swim. Her survival drive
would have propelled her to dry higher ground well before mine

had woken to any work of emergency leaving.
I wanted what mattered to me most to be believing

that I had something to lose and to lose that,
that belief. Life is the art of leaving all that

we love and what we hate without attaching
to our desire to keep things. Life is flux. But at each thin

peak between birth and dying, frail weaklings,
how hard we clutch, how fast we cling.

Flanders' Faces
WATERCOLOR AND COLORED PENCIL
ON STRATHMORE BRISTOL PAPER

LET GO, COME BACK!

Let go, let go, says the blackbird to the suet
swinging off the deck's feeder, clinging

as the shiny bird snuffles off a beakful and flaps away.

My friend sits in the recliner
he bought for his wife in her final decline

two years ago and he can't decide if he's as young
as he feels or just an old man getting old.

When she was spent with life, couldn't dance, couldn't drive,
couldn't remember one day from the next,

all she wanted was the snuck cigarettes we shared in the park.

We grew closer then than all the previous 25 years.
"You are my daughter,"

she told me, and I thought it was the cigarettes talking,

because why would she want me, broken for so many years,
for so many years no one to talk with, as her daughter?

Now he sits alone Sundays, not even a daughter
or his weekday aide to make him meals or at least smile,

so I visit and we eat pickles and we watch the downy woodpecker
puff himself, to make the coward blackbirds back away.

The suet dangles glistening in the sun, a free lunch.

I don't want him to go. I want to make him walk
twice around the block, regain his strength,

throw off the cane he struggles to stand with,
throw off the burden of his wife's long death
and come back to his ninetieth year.

In the overgrown garden, dogwood blossoms shrivel to shrouds
the dark-centered poppies let go their carnival brights.

Anguish Screaming
ACRYLIC ON PAPER

ANXIETY SPEAKING

for Joe

Tonight I'm up late, worrying
about a badly canned chestnut purée
and botulism,

a useless endeavor
since according to Merck, I'll know
soon enough

from "difficulty speaking
or swallowing . . . lassitude and weakness
progressing to paralysis."

With only 130 cases in the U.S. in a year,
it's not very likely, but as I said,
I worry,

and worry attaches
to anything:

leprosy, asteroids falling
from the sky, the dirt on your hands.

Most people worry too much about things
that don't matter and won't last.
But my friend Joe is losing
his speech to the slow dying
of Lou Gehrig's.

Six months from now,
who knows what won't work any longer
or which will matter most.

An assistive device speaks
the computerized slang of
words that he fumbling types.
But how I miss
the sound of his voice,

lost
except when I call
and his cassette machine answers:

"This is Joe speaking.
I can't come to the phone right now
but I'll call you right back
just as soon as I'm able."

Blackbird on Snow
ACRYLIC ON STRATHMORE BRISTOL PAPER

STATE PROPERTY

*Prisoners call the Washington State Penitentiary at
Walla Walla, "The Walls"
For Arthur Longworth*

The State has owned you
since you can't remember when,
body, mind and what's left of your spirit
shackled to a prison more shattering
than the Walls, where at 18 you ended your life
in the freeworld.

Hadn't The Big House
always beckoned, ever since the first time
you entered a Home and found it no refuge,
only a place so battering you ran straight
into the arms of a detention center
where at least no one pretended to care?

Who would care anyway about just another
juvenile delinquent with a mouth
to feed? It was hard to say
when mere delinquency—a word
that, defined, meant only
that you'd "left completely,"
but left what was left to the imagination,
left home, left hope behind, left off caring—
turned from trying to survive to the criminal.

Homeless, hungry, no better educated
than an arrested ten-year-old, you
stole bread, then stole something middle class
and valuable and we, nation of Inspectors
Javert, were too righteous to split hairs
and see you.

But somehow an innocent
was killed and now you are up against the wall
in Walla Walla, amidst the teem
and clangor of that crazy noise-filled space,
with no hope, no hope of freedom
and even if it kills you this time
you swear you will redeem yourself,
reclaim and save yourself from the death
of that which still remains humane
in you.

One aching brick at a time,
some walls are built, others are torn down...
Outside the canteen window,
western ospreys build their nests,
a beaver slaps the water with its tail.

Sleeping Face with Moon
ACRYLIC ON GESSOBORD

BUOYANT

The dead cross the river, swimming.

Past drowning now,
some crawl,
some leisurely sidestroke,
some float on their backs,
toes pointing toward the sky.

Who knows what lies ahead:
Tír na nÓg, Valhalla,
Island of the Seven Moons?

No one can say for sure
if there's any shore, far or near.

Some have cracked their teeth
on bitterness, believing
that to die is to lose all.

Others say there is only light
shining on the best of what used to be.

We dream, we dream and wake,
we wake and hope our dreams
mean something,
that the dead know more
than just the river
and that they must swim.

Daddy, keep your head up,
kick your feet, push the water
away.

'32 Chevy with Murmuration of Starlings
OIL PAINTING ON PAPER BONDED TO BOARD

WHEN I LOSE YOU

When I lose you,
will you remember the leaves
of my brown name?

Not like an oak, which clings
snow after snow

but like the poplar
spilling her yellow dress
to the insistent fingertips of fall

The mother of grief
is a kind forgetting

and I tell you now
that I will forget everything
I will forget even you, beloved

Remembering light
like a leaf stilled in limestone

who would have thought
we could weigh so little?

Five Watchers at the Tree of Creation
MIXED MEDIA ON PAPER

WE HAVE COME INTO THE WORLD TO SING

What if the world spoke in song
instead of with the many words
that by obfuscating divide us?

Language would then be as simple
as single octaves and all our problems
a matter of do, re, mi, fa…so
that in Teheran, if Hassan crooned
Persian love songs to his beloved,

Reba could respond in Arkansas
with plucked or hammered dulcimer
and both might understand.

Singing is the first language we learn—
filtered by the womb to solfège,
the wordless tune of rise and fall
we learn to love before we're born
and ever afterwards its prosody
prefer before all others.

All sound is music sometimes
and surely to say the hills are alive
with music is no metaphor. We may talk
to the trees and sing of our sadness

but if only we'd stop to *listen*
we'd hear their thawing xylem
tap out ecstatic Balkan rhythms
at the end of a hard winter,

rhythms magnanimous as the idea
that the universe was spun out of song,
beginning not with a Word that divides
but the vibrating A above middle C.

And tell me, now some genetic scientist
has assigned each nucleotide a musical value
so we can chant the plainsong of our genes,
like monks meditating
on the strange melody of being human,
how can we keep from singing?

LIGHT

Light, yes—
he would always remember her as light,
the way a dying leaf remembers light,
falls to the ground
and yet picks up a bit of the sun.

All beings remember light
with their bodies
and so it is his body
recalls the light over the water
recalls her skin, translucent as a medieval madonna
her eyes like small banked fires.

Now, from where he stands
at the dark forested edge of the pond
he can still feel the light of her body against his,
he can feel that light going out
when she told him she was
that dying leaf.

He didn't understand,
didn't want to understand
the migrating geese crying, *Why die? Why die?*
as they soared in the light of sunset.

Only afterwards did he see how it is
that until we die
the light never leaves completely
even when we live eclipsed lives,

the moon black against the sun
just its fiery corona left to tell us
that light is life, that light is the fire
with which we fight the earth in us,
that the soul lights even the bleakest self,
and that the body goes opaque
at the moment we lose that fight
the darkness of earth reclaiming us
when the soul departs,
only to shine elsewhere and forever.

The Birth of the Biohazard Ball
COLORED PENCIL ON STRATHMORE BRISTOL PAPER

TEN MINUTES

For Carolyn Spiro

Sometimes when you've spent hours rushing somewhere
and just as many hours rushing back
you ought to make yourself stop ten minutes from home
ten minutes short of where you can put your feet up
finally, and get out at the road's edge
stretch like a cat and ask yourself where you are
going and where have you been and why
are you hurrying just to get it over with, or is there no point
to this day but in the ending of it?
Ten minutes, this pause
wrenched out of the rush by the roadside
getting the kinks out, lets you hear the sudden quiet
of your own thoughts
as the out-of-doors pours in and gives you pause.
What have you been doing all day
racing, rushing, wasting your time all day
for what, to get what over with?
Better to have rested more along the way,
to have seen, to have been, to have watched, listened
to have paid attention
than to have beeped and swerved so much
sped and sweated in bottlenecks
and cursed the traffic for what could neither be avoided
nor its fault, being its nature.
Where had you been all day
in your hurrying to get home, but on your way
along the only way there was: yours.
Oh, but you should have known better—

how all homes are but temporary shelter:
a roadside or leafy park bench,
a ramshackle timber lean-to —
each a place to rest as good as any mansion
ten minutes away. Ten mere minutes from home
the roadside beckoned with saffron mustard sprigs,
sprays of bouncing bet. You were too much in a hurry,
no time to pay attention, so nearly home.
Oh, but you should have known better—

There are times and places we must stop
or we pay the rest of our lives.

UN/NATURAL PHENOMENA

FEBRUARY: A PEASANT'S LAMENT

*An ekphrastic poem based on the Limbourg brothers illuminated
"Book of Hours," Les Tres Riches Heures de Duc de Berry, for the
month of February*

Snow, snow, and more snow coming.
Centuries after I am mold some villein will boast
April's cruelty most severe; the fool
never sat out a cunt-curdling northern French winter,
chilblains doing what devil's work
idleness don't, even the pigeons unable
to scratch their whatall from the frozen dirt,
though ourselves, we feed fairly on their skinny carcasses
for now, I thank you kindly.
Oh, I envy the sheep their wool, the barrels
their beer, and my mistress her warm white petticoat
chastely concealing her tight cherry, while mine,
though cherry no longer, is cold, cold.
But here we share a roasting before the fire
so I flap my tunic above my knees and spread 'em,
letting blessed holy warmth
ease up my loins like a man's love.
The roof creaks and snow, the snow keeps falling.

Avenging Angel
ACRYLIC ON GESSOBORD

NATURAL PHENOMENA

Flash floods, the reports says, kill several times
more people each year than lightning

but this does not lessen my fear for my son,
on his bike, coursing casually between bolts,

delivering the evening news. I think,
calming myself with science: rubber grounds

electricity; surely a bicycle is almost
as safe as a car. The newest thrash of lightning

cracks the sky, followed by innocuous tympani, rain
pounds the open sills. Quickly I shut all the windows,

looking through the strange darkened afternoon
for my ten-year-old who is working

towards a motorized dirt bike, better, he says,
then the ten-speed I gave him, and legal

if potentially lethal, in this part of the country.
No sign. I resign myself to my book, the slow, dim waiting.

He is an intelligent child; I have taught him
about thunderstorms: surely he will not shortcut his chores

through the country club this evening.
Once, I heard, a single bolt of lightning struck

the ridgepole of a tent somewhere out in the desert,
killed its occupants, then leapt twenty feet

to electrocute a man just kneeling to kiss his son
good night under an ocean of stars. I find myself

wanting to say "in order to" as if the lightning
had sought in a planned deliberate way to eliminate

one small portion of love from the turning planet.
Some speculate that light has consciousness,

that it knows when to diffract, refract, reflect or bend,
that it even knows, instantaneously, events

that affect it on the other side of the universe. Perhaps
it is this that warns me of nature's inevitable malice aforethought:

I hear the blaze before it strikes, my hair lifts,
a bike clatters in the darkness, lit up as if from within.

LOSING WINTER

North temperate Connecticut and a heat wave
in January: 60° temperatures inside
a baffling, persistent fog
whisper: *April*, April—and our boots tramp
tread-scars in backyard mud still not frozen fast.

So many have prepared for a repeat
of past years' white tonnage:
the John Deere blower and blue antifreeze,
bags of sand, new red-handled shovels
idling against the garage wall.

Now this smoothly oiled false spring sneaks up,
enticing as a carny sing-songing his wares
on a summer midway, threatens to con twigs
into budding, to coax crocuses into erupting
from their sheathes, eliciting a melancholy
we poorly explain referring to pineals and low
wattage sunshine, octaves of healing light
as yet unavailable this dim northern season.

There is something ominous in such warmth.
The meaning of spring is winter after all,
and winter's sullen necessities:
crystal whiteness falling all day in the silver maples,
a steady blue weeping of icicles
suspended from the eaves,
steam and smoke rising in frigid columns
from stacks above the city.

It is winter after all. Not even Florida
wants the temperate tropical. Let it snow, I plead,
in the words to a song but not singing:
let it snow, let it snow, *let it snow.*

Wonder
COLORED PENCIL AND ACRYLIC ON PAPER

FRIDAY NIGHT VIGIL

*2009 vigil for 350.org, an organization dedicated
to getting the CO2 concentration in the atmosphere
down to 350 parts per million.*

Shivering in the wind, we fight to light our candles
as we gather in the darkness of an approaching storm.
But the icy blow keeps snuffing out each flicker
so we just stand, our signs alone aloft to passing traffic,
standing for the stand we take: for the changing world,
and for a last chance to change. We stand for smiling photos,
taken from across the streaming street.
One car beeps, a driver gives the V-sign in support.
But most drive on without a single word or sign
that they have heard or seen a thing, or even recognized
we're standing here for anything.
My hands freeze stiff, release their glass and candle with a crash,
a glint of shards, a splash upon the sidewalk. Someone
with safer gloves stoops to sweep the shards away...
I think, *How lovely the world is today, although it's dying.*
And though it's all we have (and lord knows, it's more
than we can handle) we stand here in this freezing dark
against the darkness and light one candle.

Sometimes a Dreamer Dreams a New Dream
Oil on Gessobord

BLACKBERRY WINTER

*"Blackberry winter" is the name given to late-spring
frost especially one that occurs after the blackberry blossoms.
It is considered a harbinger of a good crop.*

How spoiled we have been by early
mild temperatures, the calendar officially spring.

You press your face to the morose pane,
pondering the silent deliberate snowfall,

which feathers the nested crocuses white,
and pileates the trumpets of the new-born daffodils.

Even blackberry canes bow low
towards the soil they began in,

their bloom-skirts limp as ruined taffeta
retelling their history of darkness

to worms half frozen in the dirt.
Grackles squabble and scream, half-starved,

over the last of the suet you hung
in the branches of the sugar maple.

Now you see how an unexpected return
of winter can teach a painful patience,

teaches how we may be forced back two steps
for every one we move ahead,

resilient to success as to failure.
But if only I could, I would tell you

that spring did come,
that the snow melted on those stiff canes,

and the blackberries resurged
ripening to rich black thimbles,

filling your pails at summer's end
three times to overflowing.

THE SONG OF THE ANT

"For the listener, who listens in the snow . . ."
—WALLACE STEVENS

In those days I was always cold
as I had been a long time, mindful of winter
even at the solstice of my high summer days

always, always the crumb and crust of loss
and near-loss of everything held dear
before the *saison d'enfers* and the ice to come

But there was the wind
There was still the wind making music,
and I, at one with the quirky stir of air

bowing the suppliant trees
bowing the branches of those trees for the sound
of songs held long in their wood

Changes change us: rings of birth, death, another season
and we hold on for nothing and no reason
but to sing.

Consider the Bullfrog
Colored pencil on ATC

CONSIDER THE BULLFROG

Who
night and day
belches "jug-o-rum"
to a teetotaling
bog; whose noisy
lieder of drink
and bawds last all
summer long;
who nibbles
asterisks
of water striders
dimpling the surface
of the black pond
and ensnares
tangy damselflies
with the quick ribbon
of his tongue;
who after all
is not a Prince
in disguise; who
suffers himself to be
pithed for science;
who sculls
through sweet
mud in *la nostalgie
de la boue*; who
is Frog among frogs;
who needs no god;
who does not know
he will die.

Cat on the Prowl
OIL PASTEL ON STRATHMORE BRISTOL PAPER

TOOTH AND CLAW

Sufficient unto self, a feline
stalks the mouse that low has climbed
inside our trellised trumpet vines

while noisy fights break out between
the grouse that steal the haute cuisine
of kitty's costly tinned sardines

for she, much pampered, still prefers
the tang of rodent flesh and fur,
as crickets rasp and beetles whir.

With one sure leap of Grand Design
she fangs its nape and snaps its spine
'mid purslane, spurge and chamomile.

Then dainty, having dined on gore,
she drops rich tribute at my door
as if I'm her conspirator—

mouse-head and tail for me to savor,
best bits shared without a quaver
wet with blood and fresh with flavor.

Post-prandial, Cat pads round a bed
and sleeps, well-exercised and fed.
So I must do her work instead.

Whilst sun or moon hang in the sky,
That Nature's cruel, I won't deny
to make us kill and eat or die.

Ignoring all the grousing grouse,
I bring a shovel from the house
and bury what remains of Mouse.

LESSON

Listen to me, listen hard:
this is *not* where things begin.
Hammering the universe to a life
where everything seems new
is not the point.
Nor is this the radiant split second
when the earth cracks wide
with fire and steam
so like a mouth we almost
hear: Repent, repent—
The end is near!
No, we are merely fishermen,
scouring the Grand Banks
for those storied millions,
desaparecidos in the great space
between truth and rumor.

Suddenly a fish arcs the line
our battle to reel him in
an ancient one, 'til he smacks the deck
in this terrible oxygen,
the struggle over or just begun.
Why does love have to end
badly, I ask,
as flickers of rainbow spark off
its scales and it seems
to have given up life
for light. Your face in shadow,
you ask what I mean

but I cannot answer.
Maybe the fate of fish is answer
enough: Even in love
we are doomed to loss. Too late
to grant water or life,
I toss what will be
our dinner on ice.

POEMS IN WHICH
I SPEAK FRANKLY

Fork You, Psychiatry
COLORED PENCIL AND GOUACHE PAINT
ON STRATHMORE 4-PLY PAPER

TYRANNOSAURUS REX

Howard M. Spiro, MD 1924-2012

Tyrant, they called you, emperor, bully,
the first time I was in the psychiatric wing.
Yes, you finger-painted, getting down on your knees

to smear pigment with stiff abandon.
But afterward, in the hall, when I froze, contorting,
you let the whole world of the ward know

your scorn, imitating me, calling me "crazy."
I seemed finally better. I came home.
But when I failed you, leaving med school,

an embarrassment and a humiliation
who couldn't even keep work as a clerk or waitress,
you claimed suddenly you had "three children" not four.

Between us interposed silence for forty-some years
as I learned to live on $3 a day, writing my life
into poems when I had words to share.

Years passed inside "the bin" and out "on the farm,"
as I called the hospital and those programs by day
structuring my life. But hospitals dimly shape-shift

after a dozen or more and there are decades
of my life that are lost even to memory,
each melding into another like shadows

on night-lit walls in carbon paper alleys.
One keyhole through which I see the past:
Forced shock treatments' drowning anesthetic drops

and stunned awakenings. Then, somehow, there you are,
standing in the seclusion room door
resuming a conversation as if begun just yesterday

not decades years before, no older, or at least
no grayer than "Daddy" again, shorter yes but
kinder. What could I do but respond?

I never dreamed that at eighty-three
you'd lose your fire, habanero, old Nero,
or that I, Rome, would ever stop burning.

They Love You So Much You Hate Yourself
Collage

FORGETTING TO REMEMBER

*Multiples: former shorthand for people diagnosed with multiple
personality disorder, believed to arise from early sexual trauma and
abuse, now considered a dissociative disorder.*

Two suicides and such a multitude of multiples
wrung from their imagination the year I was there
by student-psychologists
eager to make names for themselves,
the halfway facility would be shut down for good the next,
but not before seeds of uncertain certainties were sown:
repressed memories miraculously recovered
from the abyss, of incests, sodomies, satanic abuses,

so even my stalwart insistence
on a happy-go-not-so-unlucky childhood
became stained by the sepia of doubt:
had I really escaped such clutches?

Knowing memory's foibles,
it's hard to trust
what my sister tells me was in fact true:
that there really were neighborhood "Bad Boys"
and a shack in the woods
where they kept a stash of comic books and pin-up calendars,

the price to read there all afternoon
if you were a girl : *a feel,*
that I'm not wrong to believe I read my fill

of "Archie" and "Prince Valiant" and "Peanuts"
inside.

Though I had to find my own way out
afterwards after they'd gone,
taking their comics with them,
leaving just "June," now unpinned from the wall

in her tiny shorts, the shine of her raspberry lips
pouting next to a tractor,
I recall only
dry motes falling through the last rays
of sun, the smoky smell of sawdust and dust,
and grit under my bare feet,
my trembling relief,
as I studied a stroll through the back door at home,
perhaps worse for the wear
but on time for supper
so nobody questioned the dirt in my hair.

Mata Otam
COLORED PENCIL ON PAPER

MENSES

For Rose W.

After it quits for good, six years later you can't
believe there are words you've clean forgotten.
Reading "flow," and "menarche," for instance,
in the book by your friend, the sociologist,
for a moment you don't understand them.

But you do understand the book's would-be beatnik,
that girl-Kerouac who couldn't light out for Mexico
or go "on the road," for lack of a carload
of Kotex, all they had in those days
to staunch a girl's flow; how many times had *you*
failed to run away in the 60's for fear
panhandling wouldn't buy Tampax?
Nothing fogged that judgment,
not even when weight loss jinxed all flow for years.

Consider your menarche at 13,
when you couldn't prevent bleeding
nor hope to conceal your becoming a woman
which was a failure much worse
than breaking an upstairs bedroom window at ten.

Confess your sin, oh, confess it now
to your mother, a woman
so clean and so good
she has never herself been stained.

No One Listens
COLORED PENCIL ON ATC

THE RAPE OF THE HUG, 2005

Rape: orig. from Latin, rapere, to seize

How
do you say no to an honest hug
from a reasonable man who likes you and wants
perhaps to love you? Does he
completely understand
how you have spent your life in institutions
and only entered the adult world at age 53?
You still have so much to learn
about being a person outside of a hospital...
Does he—does anyone?—know how dangerous
even loving human contact is?
How all contact is rape
even the gentle hugs you have
been tutored to give relatives and friends?
You only withstand them and hand them over
but you do not like them.
Though you know no harm is intended
if done, when he prolongs the hug, stands closer
and turns his head towards yours
you sense the threat
of a kiss you can't for fear of hurting his feelings
though you feel no feeling
of wanting it
refuse.

Meltdown
COLLAGE

PRELAPSE OF FAILING

The shrieking dead-wakes you
from an alongside universe (unnumbered
the ones unknown, unknowable) it's
a through-breaking marble-like membrane
and your soul separates shocked from your body
with a terrible lurch only an instant
apart before at-one-ment reasserts
the world of time that happens in that eclipse:
a cat for instance is already dead in its box,
or alive and New York underwater or not
or maybe Miami, depending on the fork
in your universe or the spoon if there is a spoon—
your front teeth resonate skintight with fear
and the shakes molar-deep,
your distracted, contortionist hands
scratching fears-ful an inch that doesn't exist.

Under Attack from All Sides
COLORED PENCIL ON STRATHMORE BRISTOL PAPER

DISTEMPER

A new pill for distempered minds leaves me myself,
untempered. Not that being less prone to tempers
is a bad thing. For instance, I no longer snap and seize
at the fluorescent shatterings of daily living.
But this placidity borders on clinical torpor
so that even daytime television
seems like a worthwhile invention,
as good a way to spend sixteen hours as any other.
I'm awake all day and all night, too conscious—
thinking, thinking, not bored, but not quite interested enough
to put my hands or mind to any enjoyable task
while a K2 of necessities goes undone:
dishes, laundry, cat litter—all insurmountable molehills.
The ancient cathode ray flickers and the talkies chatter on.
Deep in my chair, smoking away
five years of non-smoker sobriety, my drugged eyes
fix six hours on "America's Top Model"
and then on a woman heavy with twins who smiles beatified
upon her "Nineteen Kids and Counting."
A dozen should-dos fog me into lumbering up
and I aim myself towards too many goals to count,
but quickly all recede into a cave of twilight.
Time for "Junkyard Wars" on channel 101.
I sit back down, light another cigarette
and press on the remote.

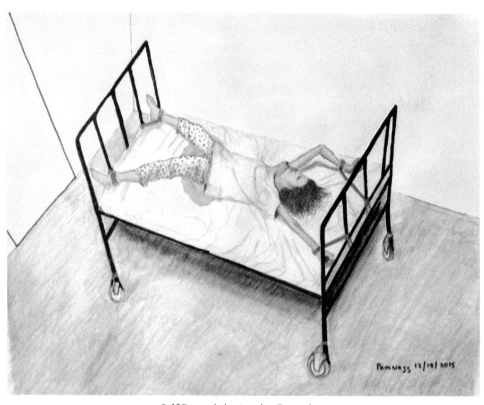

Self Portrait in 4-point Restraints
Colored pencil and gouache

POEM IN WHICH I SPEAK FRANKLY, FORGIVE ME

GOMER: ER-speak for a troublesome,
unwanted person in the emergency department,
acronym for Get Out of My Emergency Room

So many times gurneyed in by ambulance and police escort
"dangerous to self or others," and too psychotic
to cooperate or scribble consent, you suspect by now
you are just a GOMER to the snickering scrubs in the ER
who whisk you in back with the other disruptives
lying in bed, waiting for "beds."

When you dip paranoid into the inkwell of your purse
extracting a paring knife more amulet than effective protection,
they strip-search you, then, unblinking, eyeball you all night
through a bulletproof plexiglass window.
In the morning, 15-day-papered so you can't leave,
they send you ominously *upstairs.*

Later, at home, the voices decree your left leg
should go up in flames to atone for the evil within,
and you listen, and you do it, you do it:
the searing flare of cobalt actually crackles.
This time you tell no one, the char too deep for pain,
until fear of worse trumps your fear of being taken away.

This is not the story of your life.
It's *not* the story of your life—

but every time a hulking goon squad clamps restraints
around your flailing wrists and ankles, threatening
to prosecute you for biting those hands that shackle you,
you wonder if there will be any other.

Foot in Mouth
COPIC MARKERS ON PAPER

ON NOT SPEAKING

Over the seasons of my sixties
and unwillingly
suddenly silent,
no wonders spark my visual brain,
but a reason why's no wonder.

For so many years schooled
into naming everything,
words and sounds categorize the world
and wordify my senses,
precipice, for instance
with its sliced peaks
and *acrid's* encaustics, that bite on my tongue.

Even *blench*
somehow leaves me paler and more livid than before.

But there are descents into being speechless
for reasons besides pathology,
although these may not seem any reason
or even *be* reason enough to many
who believe only talking out pain aloud
makes sense.

Sensible or senseless,
I know when shutting up is preventive
or at least is less insane
than trying to be heard
by those inured to hurting
or being hurtful

when they indeed would rather hurt me
than pay heed, having heard me.

But if silence, as you claim,
overspeaks the chattering air
why do you refuse
to hear all I cannot use,
my voice to say?

Everything You Touch You Destroy
COLORED PENCIL ON STRATHMORE BRISTOL PAPER

PHILOMELA

I haven't spoken out loud for many weeks,
bullied by "voices" to a frightened into myself silence.

Still, what does "speechless" mean
in these days of text-to-speech software,
with its choice of Vikki or Samantha or Victoria voices,

especially when I'm possessed of a blog and writing fluency
enough to speak my mind to my heart's content?

Even so, being mute is not a manner of speaking.

Yet I tell you I *can* talk. Nothing physical impedes
my tongue, or locks my lips

except my brain's hallucinated snarls,
Jerry Mahoney and Charlie McCarthy thrown
into surrounding shadows

ordering up this stoppage, blockage, blockade.

Now, like Stevens' fire-fangled bird at the end of the mind
feathered unlucky, tarred, locked in golden cage

my voice remains only a memento

of everything
I wanted to say, but could not get out,
I couldn't get it out, *I could not get it out...*

Do Not Open
COLORED PENCIL ON STRATHMORE BRISTOL PAPER

REALITY CHECK

Writing prompt: Lost in the middle of nowhere

First of all, even mental patients have an address,
a 6 digit zip code and two free patient telephones,
so you're not lost in the middle of nowhere.
This isn't the movies. At least it isn't *Cuckoo's Nest*,
or the I-Never-Promised-You-a-Rose-Garden rose garden.
As for *Girl, Interrupted*? I assure you it is definitely not
that giant sleepover with hair rollers, gossip
and steaming faucet-water hot chocolate. For one thing,
hospital tap water isn't hot enough for cocoa
and unless your roommate, that anorexic
with the fruity breath and ironed tee shirts
becomes your best pal, that's it for the party—
no one else gets in your room: even in a single,
only the checker comes to disturb you: *every 15 minutes.*

Keys play a big role in film and someone always swipes
a set for the night to go AWOL or wreak havoc.
But some of the rapidly "insurance-cured" might prefer
to stay longer than shorter so going AWOL is often more
the impulsive leap through briefly opened doors
than a thoughtfully planned absconding after midnight
with a digitized keycard everyone's not so longing for.

Of course, it's sad that paranoids remain unable to trust
the good of someone's best intentions. As for the unit sociopath
having enough uninterrupted free time to wrap catatonics
in toilet tissue? The truth is there are too many groups

and too many mental health workers at work
with a job to do "and you are it, so let's get moving."
Besides, with medication and better care
catatonics are not allowed to stay that long
catatonic, so very quickly slowly they move too.

Self Portrait in Seclusion
Colored pencil on ATC

ICE HOSPITAL

Living in a hospital is like living in an Ice Hotel
where beneath the furs and fleece all the appointments
are hard frozen to the floor.
Like Ice Hotel staff, the nurses try their best
to be kind, to find compassion for those suffering
here on their sub-zero beds.
But really, they have their warm lives elsewhere.
The psychiatrist knows better. She visits briefly
once a day at the height of the sun, chewing her Vitamin D,
and encourages Hotel visitors to Happy Talk
and Life Skills. If she fails to ease their suffering
in any part, it is because she does not see it, blind
to the fact that the beds are frozen pallets that chill
to the bone. She sees only the furs and warm fleeces.
She cannot fathom why one would not rise and walk
under her cheerful ministrations after a few nights
spent on a banquette of ice. Only the aides
are savvy enough, being low-paid and long-working,
to bring in oil lanterns and hot water bottles.
The patients love them and when finally it comes time
to leave, strange how difficult it is to say good-bye
to even the hardest corner of this place.

Musée des Beaux Arts
OIL PASTEL ON STRATHMORE BRISTOL PAPER

IF WISHES WERE

Weeks she was well her friends would say she was "on the farm."
Back at the hospital was "in the bin," loony, of course, not dust

though it felt like dust, fifty years gone up in smoking—
only poems, hundreds, to show for what she might have been,

only not in this, her small failed life, where all was linked
so intimately to national disasters: guns, cold weather, Dallas

bullets, schizophrenia, O-rings—an undifferentiated all
that never should have happened it all felt her fault.

Couldn't those perverse mandarin butterflies
have stirred the air into a different turbulence, maybe

the two Kennedys or King never shot? Or, say,
the Challenger mission with all the crew jogging home

safe and sound, teacher Christa returning with her smile
to tell her class of unbelievable adventure?

If only somehow a single deadly bullet might not
have been so "magic" in 1963. That's what she dreams,

wishing between the real cigarettes and endless coffee,
or for a single O-ring not to have failed in freezing air.

GOD,
THE GREAT AVOIDER

I Am A Redbird
COLORED PENCIL ON STRATHMORE BRISTOL PAPER

DETAIL FROM MOSAIC AT SAN MARCO

"The eternity of the mosaic is a perpetual revolution, a process
that needed restarting before it was ever completed."

The Smithsonian Magazine

This is that other garden,
just some sleeping men huddled together for warmth or comfort.
The watery Venetian soil, the damp air,
have conspired to loosen the radiant tesserae
and in some places it is all illusion
a tromp l'oeil mosaic in poor paint.
Surely the secretive glassmakers of Venice expected their efforts
to last longer than this, to last an eternity.
We learn of the artisans' labors,
how flesh and cloth are imparted by stone and precious metals,
how rain, smoke and sky are marble and glass.
And we all know the story: how they fell asleep in the garden
subject to post-prandial drowsiness following
the heavy meal and the evening's celebration.
It was not really from lack of friendship or love or faith,
but they are sleeping nonetheless . . .
The gray-bearded man looks like somebody's grandfather.
Perhaps he is the fisherman. The others might be
shepherds or merchants, or even his sons.
The fisherman is leaning on his hand, as are they all,
as if in sleep still deep in thought.
A slight frown creases his brow, a hint of sadness or resignation.
Perhaps, even now, he divines in dream what is to come.

Still, nothing in this placid, luminous scene
hints at the final outcome.
Already it seems that dawn is casting its ferocious light
on their sleeping faces,
already the cup is filled,
the cock ready to crow in its appointed hour.

THE OLD STORY

My father spoke of atheism as if it were a religion,
pounding the points of his argument into the table,
spilling the salt and splitting our eardrums.
He raised me to be an atheist, too,
and I learned well the commandments of godlessness.
But at night in bed I suffered for it and was penitent,
praying prayers by the pages,
singing psalms with glosses and a litany of pleas
that somehow God would find me, small as I was,
and make me a believer,
and though a prodigal daughter
much loved, much loved.
How I longed for the sweet blow of grace
coming upon me like a hammer on a nail,
or a beggar on a penny
or raindrops on the parched red clay
turned to rust in the arid fields of my soul.

One night— I was under the covers saying the Lord's Prayer
with a lengthy meditation for each line—
my father, making the rounds, heard me.
What are you doing? he asked,
more awful than the God I longed for.
I told him, expecting punishment,
expecting a lecture on the purity of the godless intellect.
He stood a while in silence
while I waited for the one blow I didn't want.
Then he said, laughing,
you'll grow out of such foolishness, I hope.

I didn't grow out of it.
Though I never found God and stopped looking for Him
I remember my father's laughter,
the hard, cold sneer of it,
laughter at his daughter longing for God
and hoping for love
that would come like a thief in the night.

Now that I am older I know that belief
doesn't fall like a hammer
that the beggar is always penniless
and that rainfall soon evaporates returning to the cloud.
Atheism is a creed I have lived by, learned by,
and have at times been comforted by,
but if God should ever find me
I pray for foolishness.

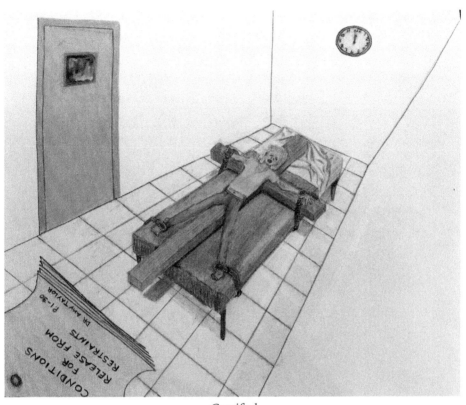

Crucified
COLORED PENCIL ON STRATHMORE BRISTOL PAPER

ABSTINENCE

sacrifice, from the Latin sacer (holy) + facere (to make)

I gave away my chair
because I had no time to sit
and only the idle rest.

I gave away my books
and I donated the bookshelves to keep

myself from self-indulgent reading.
My larder empty, the table bare,
welcome hunger came and went.

To the poorest of poor
I sacrificed my plates and pots,

lamps to the lightless, woolen socks
to whores who worked the frozen docks
at night. Clothing, clocks, leather shoes—

so much of the world to be stripped away—
I needed nothing but God
the Great Avoider.

Sometimes my head caught fire
and mystery sailed me off in shimmers
but it was all too much.

I could not sleep while others wept
or crouched in terror in the dark.

After I gave all to those with none,
there was nothing left
but my wasted body pared to bone.

How gladly was I shed of useless flesh,
the thorn that pricked
my conscience till it bled.

Now I can be one with you
in straits in prison,
and with you, on the front lines,
and one with all of you
whose names I'll never know.

I will eat no more
than your short rations
or none at all if you have none.

And if I die, as some of you will surely die
who have I been but the least of all

one small believer,
despairing of a loving God,
loving God.

Chained Burka Liberty
OIL PASTEL ON STRATHMORE 4-PLY

AFTERWARDS, WHAT THE MOTHER SAID

I was happy when those green birds
flew shining into my garden.

I thought it meant that Allah had smiled
and fate would be kind.
But the grindstone turned.

For my son, the struggle was all. I did not know
the meaning of his great determination
to be *al shaheed al hayy*, "the living martyr."

The small birds clung to the line
for nearly an hour

before they hurled themselves to the sky
in a great shrill.

Now I can think only of the gore
of innocents on a shredded shirt
I'd washed the night before,
the blood on his Quran left on a bench nearby.

I was ashamed when asked
to claim him as my child.

You ask me
am I happy my son has joined the martyrs?
Do I rejoice to be the mother of a hero?

Who cares of heroes or martyrs
I have lost my son.

May those whom he murdered forgive me.

Inshallah, we will not meet again,
no, not even in Paradise.

But had I known of his plans
I would have taken a blade, sliced open my heart
and crammed him deep inside.

I would have seamed it tight to seal him in.
I would have never let him go.

DREAM FRAGMENT 1

We were swimming across a lake.
We? But I was alone,
a pair of guileless eyes brimming
in the lake both familiar yet unknown.
God speaks in dreams, someone said
but I couldn't swim.

The lake was all, a vision
not there, not here,
my impossible buoyancy granted like grace,
and she beside me synchronizing
stroke by stroke to that far shore.

There was a house with many rooms,
some bread, a chalkboard.
Lessons arranged themselves like flowers.
To be is to mean.

Later I understood
how certain baptisms can kill

how even bread has its time and place,
is consumed in sacrifice,
making the dreamer and her dream
holy.

DREAM FRAGMENT 2: HOW TO FLY

I'm flying with a man I don't trust
in daylight

but I like the way he cheekily calls
me, "Pammy,"

as if I've always known him.

It's a school dream, but one without anxiety
because finally I'm at the top of the class,

I'm on time for the final exam,
and magically I morph into the teacher.

I teach children to fly in church.

The Unitarians in their jeans and flannels
wait in the pews on the floor,
saying, Only Catholics can fly.

Nonsense! I say, Hindus, Buddhists and you too
can fly. Just think of angels!

Then whoosh! They are aloft.

Only the pious French choirboys
remain earthbound, clutching their psalters.

In their white lace, their crimson robes,
they divest themselves furiously
in the balcony below.

Crucified #2
Colored pencil on ATC

ARTICLES OF FAITH

Black ice.
An accident's chain-
reaction crumples 28 cars
one by one.

Forgetting the latest advisory
you steer into our skid
on the frictionless slick
missing collision
by the merest sleet needle.

It's night, your panicked face
glows dashboard green
licked with gold as we pass
streetlights in cold review.

God, you say,
must be watching out
for us, meaning you and me
and this battered '92 Chevy
still too good to let go.

I remind you about all the cars
accordioned in the whiplash of impact.

Was God *not* watching out for them
or worse, deliberate in his neglect?

But this is not a theological poem.
I know nothing is guaranteed
save that none of us will survive our lives
and I'm just another nonbeliever,
whistling fear into the void.

The wreckage behind us,
we're wowed breathless by the nearness
of our miss

and though there remains
the matter of the crushed 28
I am appalled into gratitude.
As our heartbeats steady, you drive on.

Yet, despite my doubt
I can't refrain from muttering,
a faithless "Thank God!"
to still my shaking hands.

What's Bugging Me
COLORED PENCIL ON PAPER

TIME AND AGAIN

*"This world is an ever-living fire, in measures being kindled
and in measures going out. "*
ATTRIBUTED TO HERACLITUS

You ate us all, Father of the Universe,
God, Time, Ground of our being—
fearing rumors of Zeus and of Eden,
trembling at a serpent's offering
your pomegranate, forbidden fruit,
fearing the gate to the world you'd have to open,
pushing us through so human history
could finally begin.

Who would have thought
we'd be such a heavy stone in the belly
you'd have to spew us out just to end the pain?
All-Pitiable, didn't you know that fear of pain
is but shorthand for the fear of annihilation?

Every evening at sunset darkness brought panic
for how real were you if none could see you,
how could you exert your power?
A secret tree grew in the dark, but you never knew
the seed it bore nourished our freedom.

We were, in the end, no Titans, we were only women
and men. Our needs and griefs were small
once we were sure we would live and breed.
But though we had our mothers to support
and our mountain chalets to thatch, we knew
history would need us. Rolling out of your throat

we made straight for the epic poets,
story-makers who could kindle conflagration
within every living thing.

God Strikes Down An Ant
COLORED PENCIL AND COPIC MARKER
ON STRATHMORE BRISTOL PAPER

PRAYERS OF THE PEOPLE

Worship wasn't always so private:
davening mortal with God alone together
like children whisper-plotting a prank, but secretly.
There was rank animal sacrifice in the public square,
the perfect spring lamb and competition for tithes,
honest bribery buying God's good graces,
good crops, prosperity, the High Priest's arcane
ritual slaughter, which was enacted *on* stage.
Yes, God was a harsh taskmaster in those days,
demanding the first and the best
of all we'd sweated and bled for: bountiful
harvest, cattle, and if called for, our eldest children.
But we trusted this God with whom we'd bargained.
A dollar was a dollar and we got what we paid for.
Now things have changed. We pray alone.
Our secrets lift in subtle vapors, no meaty smell
of burnt offerings to please a mammal god.
Our prayers are mere pheromones of aggression
or desire, prayers like bluffs, prayers that hint
much more than they state, still thinking a feint
could force God to fold or lay all His cards on the table.

Sometimes You Can't Help But Scream
COLLAGE

DOUBTING

In the Baptist church the choir sings "Just As I Am"
while youngsters in white wait for dunking
as unprepared as I am for the frigid water,
the heart-deep chill that shudders the bones,
seals the blood up tight in its vaults.
I have come to be baptized, to accept Jesus
as Lord and Savior and be saved in the name
of the Father, Son and Holy Spirit. It's Easter Eve.
I feel like Cinderella in my white dress
and wonder if I shall wake up a charwoman.
The minister wears plaid swim trunks
under robes that float up around his middle like a dress.
His hairless legs are bleached as bone. I hate him.
He smiles at me as I trudge down into the tank
and grips me by the hand, one arm about my back
as if he thinks I won't make it on my own.
A baby in the church begins to squall.
Someone coughs and coughs. The choir sings
the wrong hymn, the clock strikes the hour
and I hold my nose and go under.

AFTER FAILURE

He is going home, a long way.
He has told no one.
No one will suspect
his departure three hours before
his absence is noted.

And no one will be waiting
at the other end
with a seasonal coat or umbrella,

ready with a false smile, the rigorous
cheer of good manners
that will keep him from telling his secret
for many long weeks.

After where he's been
the snow is merely picturesque
and cold.

In the taxi he will take to his old house
the driver will tell him more
than he wants to hear

about Jesus loving him, yes,
the nobody only God could love.
It is some important holiday

he no longer celebrates,
Thanksgiving, perhaps.
He will ask to be dropped a few blocks away

and will go the rest on foot,
wishing to appear hearty

before those who are still counting on him
to make good
in the soap opera
of their lives. But now

here he is at the door
he doesn't need to knock at, knocking,
the twenty-four karat surprise.

Opening, his mother begins her big smile—
he's her best news all day—
as he steps uncertainly into the dark
of the one life to live
he has left to live.

Big-eyed Child with Red Hat
ACRYLIC ON STRATHMORE BRISTOL PAPER

LOTUS

Be fat and green and still,
little jade Buddha of my heart,
broken by love in my thirteenth summer.
Is it possible to want nothing more
than to want nothing more perfectly?
Smoke of sandalwood rising dreamy
amid the burn of tallow candles,
flowers of a white light
fractured into color, pomegranates
globed and teeming—*maya*—
to not want all this?
And if I one day wake, not
wanting anymore what I thought I always
wanted, let me not contemn
the lush seductions of commerce
and the useful body.
For the world, it seems, is always too much,
its prescient polar looming
a dream of shifting green water,
snow blown hard against the door.

POEM FOR REGINALD, CHRISTMAS 1985

It is winter, four o'clock in the afternoon.
A drunk man, not yet dead on his feet,
accosts me, says,
"Hey, are you a college girl?"
I am not a student anymore—
It has been years since I went by bells
from room to room,
scribbled frantic exams
in booklets bound in blue.
I look young, I know that. My hair is not
yet gray, and perhaps that is why
he asks the question.

"I read books, too," he tells me,
falling into step beside me
though he had met me coming the opposite way
and I am hurrying to be out of Dutch Point by nightfall.
He walks me all the way up to Main Street,
accompanying me through the backyards of tenements
past lounging men who might have wished me
less than well.
Though he insists on staying on the street side
like a gentleman, some primitive fear
urges me to shift my purse
to my other shoulder.

He is a genius he tells me, and I believe him,
but he is an alcoholic and his breath smells
as if he has been drinking.
Still, I am not afraid of him

and when he asks, I tell him my name.
There is something sad about him.
He says he thinks I can cure him,
could marry him.
His name is Reginald.
He speaks like an old friend
and suddenly I am lonely too.

That is all. There is no moral to this tale.
I am thirty-five, single, childless,
and lonely
as a drunk man
offering me company at Christmastide.
We come to my building. He leans closer.
When he hugs me
I hold on *tight*.

LEARNING
TO SEE
IN THREE
DIMENSIONS

HARD PLACES

Women understand
the pillar of Lot's nameless wife,
how though she knew Sodom was home
to every vice and vogue
she still wanted to stay, a mother
of young children, the tired wife of the tired-
of-traveling Willy Loman
Lot had become, a failure in all eyes
but hers, and when she turned
her head to glance back at the big city
shrinking behind them,
wanting to fix it in memory,
she knew she could never leave.

Using Klimt: The Kiss
COLLAGE

HELEN

Before: embarrassing to admit we too were taken
by that face flaunting its loveliness wherever
we turned our crow's-feet and indeed it was difficult
to turn away from the headlines in the stalled checkout line
at the market where the girl subtracted someone's over-budget
hamburger. Embarrassing to admit we ate it up, ate
our hearts out, greedy for the inside dope
behind the front page, as hooked as anyone
but too much the snobs to be seen in public
feasting on it: failed suicide, bulimia, self-loathing
perfectionism so like our own but not for once our own,
this just another lucred-lovely, yet one of us beneath
all the glittered privilege. Oh, she couldn't fool us:
all along we knew even that face would fall, wrinkle, sag
and bag, aging just like ours, given time.

Afterward, what more could be said? Yet
too much was said and not enough faithful to the original,
a version too delicate or indelicate, too dangerous
for public consumption, as if in acquiescing to the whitewash
we would never continue to believe otherwise.
As if we could ever forget her nights alone in the regal pantry
gorging, weeping, purging—forget cries for help scorned
as crying wolf, willful hysteria, a public embarrassment.
Maybe, after all that, she couldn't win, but how we wanted her to,
wish she had, hope she did in the end before the end,
the tabloids getting it right at last in "The Kiss,"
our fairy tale heroine having the time of her life
once upon a time before her time ran out.

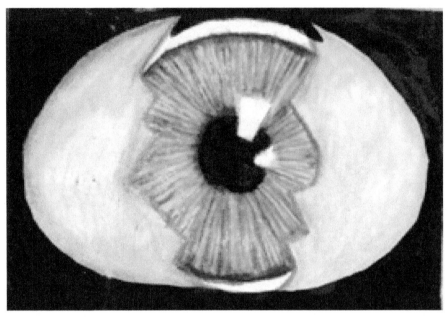

Eye in the Egg: Birth of Insight
COLORED PENCIL ON ATC

DUMB LUCK

Say this fictional man survives a disaster
that claimed too many for him to sleep
peacefully or doing nothing return
to his life unchanged.
The plane crash,
his *kairotic* moment,
is a Freudian fulcrum
around which all he has or will become
pivots,
it's like the pinprick in the pupil
of a black hole that nothing can escape,
or the simmering quiet eye of a hurricane,
center between destruction and destruction.
How much closer than we can imagine
lurk so many of fate's reminders
that survival's not as simple as walking away
though we'll say he does walk away
because worse has already come to the worst
possible, and nothing will ever be the same
on the whole map of god's wormy dirt,
which opened a grave to take him in
then, inconceivably, spared him for nothing.

Girl with Blue Hair
WATERCOLOR ON ARCHES WATERCOLOR PAPER

LABOR DAY BLUES

You will remember her blue hair
the rest of your life, that improbable indigo,
blue as the high burning stars
blue as the canopy of Greek skies
over the Acropolis in summer.
Here the flowering *Myosotis* sends its blue curls
across the river bank, naming itself
with a wry hope: *Forget-me-not*—
Do you remember the blue spruce with its pewter
needles, the bluestar grass in its shadow
and the shadows themselves,
their blue silence? Do you recall
how a black girl's skin blues to nacre
in that languid slant of twilight, descending
to a navy darkness pricked by stars?
Surely you will never forget her—
the drowned girl at the Labor Day picnic
in her blue pinafore, how she counted
crossing step by step the wet blue stones.
Did she dream the beryl water
before she stumbled?
You recall only the tinsel, the marching bands
their intricate dance steps while they played.
Did you hear how smooth their segue
from Sousa into the blues?

OVERPOPULATION

There are too many dead
bodies for the local cemetery,
children and children's children
squeezed out of the family plot,
limbs and ribs encroaching as their bodies
fold unnaturally to conserve
precious space beneath the grass.

Others overlap in a boundary dispute
between neighbors
who have long since forgotten
their own quiet names.

A disturbance of heavy equipment—
backhoes and jack hammers—
jars the hard ground
as a new mausoleum goes up and up
in the last half-acre left, zoned
for a coffin condominium,

tripling capacity by doubling
and quadrupling up the dead
who will lie in state in a gleaming black
U of granite, inner walls
faced with pink-veined marble

names upon names stacked and inscribed,
birthdays without deathdays

as the still-living sign up for limited space,
getting dibs on their final estate
on a first gone, first come basis.

Eemie, RIP
OIL PASTEL ON STRATHMORE BRISTOL

WHOM IS IT REALLY WE KILL?
OF WHOM IS IT REALLY WE DREAM?

Is it only two years the little cat's dead now?
She persists
not in an innocent's dream
but at my door, so real

I can feel her fur in my tears.
Whoever called the injections
by which we kill our animals "sleep"
had no conscience.

Euphemisms hide facts
but they do not change them, for surely
if my brain believed there was good in her death,

Eemie would not reappear like Banquo's ghost,
reproaching with her presence

telling me truths I already know:
Even cats can die of loneliness
and she had had enough of being left to fend for herself.

Of course, there was food and water,
but after my father's death,
she gave up waiting for some density of me
to return, to connect.

Then she gave up wanting even food.
And when her liver failed

it was too late for anyone's love to save her.

But what of her last look-around at the stainless world?
How could I think it curiosity,
that sudden raised head,

when it was only a reflex to euthanasia?
How could I not understand such plain table truth?
I asked the vet how long it would take.
"She's already gone," the vet said.

The Green Monster of Psychiatry Enslaves the Helpless
COLORED PENCIL ON STRATHMORE BRISTOL PAPER

TIME-BANK POEM

Dear R, you who have asked me,
via my Service Offer ("I write personal poems"),
to "create" you a poem, can't know,
when my second late night email
fails to elicit a prompt response,
how my certainty of rejection hammers me
into old penances, how I tinfoil walls
and barricades against my extruded poisons.
Then when your emails resume the next day
mentioning your little white house,
a she-owl who watches you with soulful eyes
and your growing "sense of despair"
I imagine a woman of mature years,
alone, though perhaps through choices
not always made freely. So to meet you
I navigate unfamiliar and unpaved roads
parking behind a half-built barn
and a muddy old green Subaru.
Younger than I expect, you've moved here
to escape precisely what we never discuss.
You reference only the need for peace of mind,
and a relief from startling triggers.
Nevertheless, I understand your need to know
that spirit-familiar, the barred she-owl, *Strix varia*,
roosting on a white pine bough
outside your window all winter,
less guardian than too starving to move away
or predate the small animals atop the ice layer
between her and proper voles held in safety beneath.

Only when deep-freeze breaks in early March
and a shadow swoops silently across your pane,
do you know who's won the battle,
and cheer for a raptor's kill that saves her life.
The world, after all, is all about killing or being eaten,
which is true even in the human world
where your neighbors stalk you with barking dogs,
and talk nights, beneath your bedroom window
of that woman next door, who is not like them,
with her window salad garden and that owl.
Fearful, blind, they believe that hoot owls
harbinger death. Instead you try to see
the way a mythical Owl might see,
through cold and black of night
for clarity, for lucency, for whatever it is
that warms the living embers
and rem-embers your mind to peace.

We See it All But Shhhhh
COLORED PENCIL ON STRATHMORE BRISTOL PAPER

LEARNING TO SEE IN THREE DIMENSIONS

with thanks to Susan Danberg, Glastonbury, CT

In vision therapy, she says to think
of the eyes as if on string:
your mind must haul them together
hand over hand to see a round world.

Can you make red and green
become one color,
without losing fall or spring?

To see straight,
you must go crooked
cross your eyes a little,

and look into the corners of the world,
see what is hidden there:

sometimes a face
will float up in the emptiness.

Before the mind's eyes
can see as one,
your right finger must become two

and move as two and feel as two
though it is still only one finger.

Soon you will understand
the secret: how space, embodied,
loves all that it touches.

Yes, a hand reaching out
is a thing of beauty, yes.

Have you seen the trees
for the forest, the bright ones in front
and those in the dark farther on?

They whisper: there is no negative space,
only a shapely void, delicate
as a squash or a pale Arctic lemming.

The full bowl of day spills
into evening.

Let your eyes fill
with all that is left behind,
adoring everything hollow.

NOTES

"We Have Come Into The World to Sing"
Title is derived from a similar title by Sufi poet, Hafiz.

"Ecstatic Balkan rhythms" refers to the BBC documentary *The Rhythm of Life with Sir George Martin* where an accelerated tape recording of trees in early spring revealed regular tapping noises that echo the ⅞ rhythm of certain Balkan folk dances. It turns out that these extraordinary sounds are the thawing and popping of frozen xylem, the dead cells making up water-bearing tubules in woody plants.

"Vibrating A above middle C" refers to A440, concert pitch, the standard tuning frequency.

"Stevens' fire-fangled bird" is a reference to "Of Mere Being" by Wallace Stevens.

"Philomela"
In the Greek myth, Philomela is raped and has her tongue cut out by Tereus, the husband of her sister Procne. Rendered mute, Philomela weaves a tapestry detailing the crime to inform her sister, who, enraged, takes revenge on Tereus. At the end of the story, both Procne and Philomela are transformed into birds. In some versions of this story, Philomela turns into a female nightingale, while in others she becomes a swallow. However, neither of these birds can sing.

Jerry Mahoney and Charlie McCarthy are two famous American ventriloquists' dummies.

ACKNOWLEDGMENTS

"Poem In Which I Speak Frankly, Forgive Me" appeared in *Headspace*, Issue #1 Wesleyan University, Middletown, CT; also in *Schizophrenia is Merely a Word*, ed. David Holloway, U.K.

"Light" and "Detail from Mosaic at San Marco" were published in *Tunxis Poetry Review*, Spring 1987.

"Tyrannosaurus Rex," "Distemper," and "Ice Hospital" also appeared in *Schizophrenia is Merely a Word*, ed. David Holloway, U.K.

"The Old Story" and "Poem for Reginald" were published in *Tunxis Poetry Review*, Vol 7, Farmington, Connecticut.

"Counterfactuals" and "Learning to See in Three Dimensions" appeared in *Collective*, 2014.

"Mosaic" was published in *VPS Counterpoint*, Summer 2015, Rutland, Vermont.

"Lotus," "Blackberry Winter," and "Consider the Bullfrog" appeared in the *Three Poets* edition of *Tunxis Poetry Review*, Vol 15, Farmington, Connecticut.

CPSIA information can be obtained
at www.ICGtesting.com
Printed in the USA
LVOW05s1048190717
541749LV00002B/3/P